6. You shall not commit adultery.

7. You shall not steal.

8. You shall not bear false witness against your neighbor.

9. You shall not covet your neighbor's wife.

10. You shall not covet your neighbor's possessions.

Exodus 20:1-17
Deuteronomy 5:6-21

Originally published as
I Comandamenti, copyright © 1993
Editoriale Jaca Book spa, Milan.

English translation copyright © 1994
by Wm. B. Eerdmans Publishing Co.
255 Jefferson Ave. S.E., Grand Rapids, Mich. 49503

Printed in Italy

Library of Congress Cataloging-in-Publication Data

Biffi, Inos.
[Comandamenti.   English]
The Ten commandments / text by Inos Biffi ; illustrations by Franco Vignazia.
p.   cm.
ISBN 0-8028-3758-1
1. Ten commandments—Juvenile literature.
2. Christian ethics—Catholic authors—Juvenile literature.
3. Catholic Church—Doctrines—Juvenile literature.
[1. Ten commandments.   2. Ethics.   3. Conduct of life.
4. Catholic Church.]   I. Vignazia, Franco, ill.
BV4656.B5413   1993
241.5'2—dc20   93-39147
                                                              CIP
                                                              AC

Imprimatur
in Curia Arch. Mediolani die 4 Novembris 1992
Angelus Mascheroni
provicarius generalis

INOS BIFFI is Professor of Medieval and Systematic Theology at the
Theological University of Northern Italy, Milan.

FRANCO VIGNAZIA lives in Italy and is an illustrator, painter, and
sculptor. He also teaches art in the secondary schools.

Unless otherwise indicated, all Scripture quotations are from the New American Bible,
© 1986 Confraternity of Christian Doctrine, Washington, D.C.

The Ten Commandments

Text by Inos Biffi

Illustrations by Franco Vignazia

WILLIAM B. EERDMANS PUBLISHING COMPANY
GRAND RAPIDS, MICHIGAN

Introduction

This book on the Commandments, which follows those on the Creed and the Sacraments, uses both words and images to attempt to explain to youngsters how a Christian is to behave. Children will need the guidance of parents or other adults close to them to help them understand the text and

illustrations, and, most important, to offer them conviction, instruction, and inspiration by example.

Indeed, the parents will be the first teachers of the Commandments. They will foster in their children the desire for the Law of the Lord. Together they will enroll in the school of Jesus, the only true teacher and model, who said of himself, "I am the light of the world. Whoever follows me will not walk in darkness, but will have the light of life" (John 8:12).

God's Law for Us

When God created Adam and Eve, he gave them a conscience so that they could tell right from wrong, and he gave them the gift of freedom so that they could love and choose goodness, although they could also choose evil. In fact, in the beginning, Adam and Eve disobeyed God and by doing that chose evil, which clouded their hearts. By freely and consciously choosing evil, they sinned against God. But God has not abandoned humanity because of this sin, which is what we call original sin. Indeed, as a sign of his continuing covenant with us, he gave Moses two tablets of stone with the Ten Commandments carved on them. Jesus renewed this ancient Law in a profound way by coming down to earth and dying on the cross. He proclaimed and imprinted on the hearts of his disciples the new Law of the Gospel, which says that we are to love God and love our neighbor.

I am
the Lord
your
God.

I. You
shall
not
have
other gods
besides
me.

There is only one Lord, in three persons: the Father, the Son, and the Holy Spirit. He created us and saved us; he sees the intimate parts of our souls; he follows us constantly with love; he waits for us to come to him so that he can give us eternal joy. Whoever pretends to be God is only a false idol who deceives us and enslaves us.

We respond to the love of God by loving him and praying to him with all our hearts. Prayer is made up of three things: adoration, in which we recognize and praise the Lord as the only God; thanksgiving, through which we acknowledge his gifts to us; and respectful humility, in which we ask for God's help in faith.

There are two kinds of prayer: those we say privately, in our personal devotions at home; and those we say in Church, together with the other disciples of Jesus. This second kind of prayer is called liturgical prayer: it is the source of and model for all our

prayers. The Lord Jesus is always present in prayer.

2. You shall not take the name of the Lord, your God, in vain.

God himself revealed his name to Moses, the leader of the Hebrew people. In this way he showed his love for all humanity and his continuous presence with them.

The name of God is a sacred name: it is not to be said in vain, thoughtlessly and without respect, as if it were just any name. One must not swear to something by calling God as a witness unless it concerns a very important matter. Whoever insults God or curses him commits the sin of blasphemy.

We are to use the name of God reverently during prayer and worship. When we call upon God, we are to offer him our praise and express our gratitude and our love, still remembering the warning of Jesus: "Not everyone who says to me, 'Lord, Lord,' will enter the kingdom of heaven, but only the one who does the will of my Father in heaven" (Matt. 8:21).

3. Remember to keep holy the sabbath day.

Since the time of the apostles, the holy day for Christians is Sunday, which we call the "Day of the Lord." Because Jesus was resurrected on Sunday, the Church chose this day among all other days of the week and made it special. On this day we are to celebrate Holy Communion, engage in charitable acts, restore our spirits, and rest our bodies.

Whoever is without a serious reason for not participating in the Sunday Mass, and who spends this day like any other, seeks amusement im-moderately, and shows no interest in the welfare of others has not sanctified this holy day.

4. Honor your father and your mother.

According to the divine design, children are born into a family, from the love between mother and father. In giving life to their children, parents reveal and imitate the goodness and the creative power of God; the children carry within themselves the image of Jesus, the Son of God; and the love that binds the whole family together reflects the love of the Holy Spirit himself, which unites the Father and Jesus.

Mothers and fathers are called to educate their children with sweetness and firmness, especially by setting a good example. They help their children to grow in freedom, to discover their vocation, and to become responsible adults active within the Church and society.

Children express their thanks by obeying their parents and showing them respectful love and care. In particular, they do not neglect their parents when they are old, but remain close to them and assist them lovingly.

5. You shall not kill.

God has created us in his image and likeness, and for this reason the life of every person is sacred. Life deserves love and care from the moment it first flickers in a mother's womb until it is extinguished by death. Whoever kills another person imitates the sin of Cain, who killed his brother Abel. But whoever loves others imitates Jesus, who gave his life for us. We must do more than obey the command not to kill, however, we must protect human life and avoid any exploitation, manipulation, or domination of it. Love must come from the heart; it expels hate, jealousy, and envy, and nourishes instead feelings of goodness and forgiveness.

The legitimate defense of human life, both our own and others', is right and proper. What is wrong is suppressing innocent lives, being vengeful, and being aggressive. It is also wrong to take one's own life, because life is a gift of God.

6. You shall not commit adultery.

God made man and woman with an attraction for each other, so that they may join together in marriage, love each other, and give life to children through the intimate sharing of their hearts and their bodies. This commandment condemns unfaithfulness between husband and wife and forbids every impure thought, desire, and act. The bond of marriage requires that husband and wife honor their commitment to each other by sharing their bodies only with each other. Indeed, each of us is to respect and honor our body as a gift from God and a sign of love. The body of a Christian is sanctified by the Holy Spirit's dwelling within it, as within a temple.

7. You shall not steal.

Stealing means taking away what belongs to another person. God forbids stealing because he is concerned that the goods of the earth be divided justly, so that all people can have what they need to live with dignity, as men and women.

Those who do not adequately pay the people who work for them and those who keep so much wealth that they force others to endure in poverty, hunger, unemployment, underdevelopment, and inhuman conditions disobey this commandment. In the same way, this commandment is broken by those who get rich at the expense of the community and do not contribute to the good of that community, and by those who earn their living dishonestly and take advantage of others.

8. You shall not bear false witness against your neighbor.

Jesus said of himself, "I am the Truth" (John 14:6), and he called the devil "a liar and the father of lies" (John 8:44).

If we want to imitate Jesus, we must reject every form of falsehood. We must not deceive, cheat, or lie. We must love truth, and we must search for it with commitment and speak it with courage, even if it means making a sacrifice. We must strive to be pure, loyal, sincere, and discreet. We must not believe everything we hear, and we must keep the promises we make and keep the confidences that others entrust to us. And we must always remember the admonition of Jesus: "Let your 'Yes' mean 'Yes' and your 'No' mean 'No,' that you may not incur condemnation" (James 5:12).

9. You shall not

We have already seen that in the beginning God created man and woman so that they would be united by a faithful and enduring love and, through marriage, would form a family. They would join together in a sacred union to pass on life to their children, whom they would love and educate in the ways of God.

covet your neighbor's wife.

Marital love is especially sacred between two Christians, because their union was consecrated by Jesus with a sacrament. For this reason, God prohibits desiring another person's spouse, thinking of that man or woman as an object to be possessed. He severely condemns whoever tries to break the union between husband and wife. And Jesus has added, "Everyone who looks at a woman with lust has already committed adultery with her in his heart" (Matt. 5:28).

10. You shall not covet your neighbor's possessions.

In the last commandment, God warns us not to envy the possessions of others, thus not fostering in our hearts the love of riches. Those people who are anxious to acquire earthly goods become slaves to material things; they become selfish and insensitive to the needs of others; they commit unjust acts simply to possess certain objects.

Jesus did not choose a life of luxury for himself; he chose a life of poverty and simplicity. And he proclaimed that the poor are blessed because they are saved from the dangers of wealth. Let us listen to his words: "Do not store up for yourselves treasures on earth. . . . But store up treasures in heaven. . . . What profit would there be for one to gain the whole world and forfeit his life?" (Matt. 6:19-20; Matt. 16:26).

The Beatitudes

Blessed are the poor in spirit,
for theirs is the kingdom of heaven.

Blessed are they who mourn,
for they will be comforted.

Blessed are the meek,
for they will inherit the land.

Blessed are they who hunger and
thirst for righteousness,
for they will be satisfied.